We Don't Know We Don't Know

We Don't Know We Don't Know

Poems

Nick Lantz

Graywolf Press

Publication of this volume is made possible in part by a grant provided by the Minnesota State Arts Board, through an appropriation by the Minnesota State Legislature; a grant from the Wells Fargo Foundation Minnesota; and a grant from the National Endowment for the Arts, which believes that a great nation deserves great art. Significant support has also been provided by Target; the McKnight Foundation; and other generous contributions from foundations, corporations, and individuals. To these organizations and individuals we offer our heartfelt thanks.

Published by Graywolf Press
250 Third Avenue North, Suite 600
Minneapolis, MN 55401
All rights reserved.

www.graywolfpress.org

Published in the United States of America

ISBN 978-1-55597-552-4

2 4 6 8 9 7 5 3 1
First Graywolf Printing, 2010

Library of Congress Control Number: 2009933821

Cover design: Kapo Ng @ A-Men Project

For Vicky

Contents

Introduction

"No fool," says the clown in *Twelfth Night*: I am merely a "corrupter of words." Some four centuries later, when bad-faith deployments of language appear to outnumber the good, when doublespeak and obfuscation thrive, when inquiry is trumped by foregone conclusion, and the instruments of inquiry, words above all, are made to suffer systematic corruption, what is a worker-in-words to do? Nick Lantz, a worker-in-words extraordinaire, has taken his title, and his brief, from one of the low points in American public discourse: from Donald Rumsfeld's justification of the war in Iraq. And in a project that begins where political satire leaves off, he has made that sorry debasement an incitement to the better speech, the sharper thinking, the clearer analogies and juxtapositions that can be its only antidote. Rumsfeld presides as something of a fallen muse in *We Don't Know We Don't Know,* his bland evasions recruited again and again as epigraphs for poems designed to contest his reign. And, in a wonderfully witty juxtaposition, he is made to share the (epigraphic) limelight with Pliny the Elder, the first-century natural philosopher whose astute comments on the limits of human understanding provide a tonic corrective to intellectual pride. Is this the first time Donald Rumsfeld and Pliny the Elder have entered into dialogue? If so, the meeting is long overdue. Pliny compares our powers of reason, unfavorably, to that of the bees. Of all living creatures, writes Pliny, only man "knoweth nothing unlesse he be taught."

We like to think we're teachable. New leadership and a cathartic election have restored some of our immediate hopes for America. But hope is not the work of a moment. Lantz has his eye on the long haul: how deeply, how steadily we must probe the fonts of feeling and thought if we are to address the afflictions that all-too-chronically ail us. Which is where the power of his poems comes in.

"God was only ever as big as the hole we saw him through," says the leper who was not allowed inside the church, who could only follow the elevation of the host by the sound of a bell and the view through a crack in the wall. The poem continues, in second voice:

> The bee's eye comprises thousands of hexagons.
> The eye inscribes its pattern on the mind, and for this

reason Plato loved the bee, it six legs and six-sided
dreams. No bee ever thought to build a honeycomb
Of three- or five-sided chambers.

(“'The order that Bees keepe in their worke'”)

Juxtaposition. Distillation. The cadence of story and the cadence of appre-
hension. Poetry does its thinking by just such musical means. Of difficult
subjects—the structures of cognition, the structures of social exclusion, the
promptings to love—Nick Lantz writes with elegant simplicity. Most poets
take a lifetime to learn as much.

He is also a master of the image:

Beyond the blue chalk line
of the highway, acreage
of corn, stalks cuckolding
one another in the wind.

I shall never think of airborne pollination in the old way again.

And here in the kitchen
the dishwasher jet thuds
its muted round, too like
the sonogram heartbeat.

(“Lightly at First, Then Rapture”)

This last move, into the sonogram heartbeat, conveys something of
Lantz's delicate way with emotional through-line and personal narrative.
“'Of the Parrat and other birds that can speake'” affords a fuller example.
The poem begins with a hilarious assertion from Pliny's natural history
and an equally hilarious anecdote about a parrot and an aging mother
(possibly the speaker's, possibly someone else's). Perfect comic timing,
perfect idiomatic capture. And as the poem proceeds, behold, a trans-
formation. The deadpan comedy of mental decline (misplaced objects,

misplaced words) becomes the moving story of, well, of mental decline. And of the mother's death:

> "When you
>
> drive home that night with the cage
> belted into the passenger seat, the bird
> makes a sound that is not a word
> but that you immediately recognize
>
> as the sound of your mother's phone
> ringing, and you know it is the sound
> of you calling her again and again,
> the sound of her not answering.

Acuity of mind is not enough. Like any true poet, Nick Lantz makes room for the heart as well.

How many are the paths of our undoing? Some casual:

> Last
> weekend, you wandered
> into the swale behind
> your house and caught
> two teenagers hammering
> railroad spikes into a tree.
>
> ("'Of Swine, and their nature'")

Some orchestrated. Of the unfinished Ryugyong Hotel, North Korea:

> The postage stamps depict a completed hotel
> but were issued before the building was half
> finished. Today, to post a letter with such
> a stamp is an act of sedition.
>
> ("'Of the last peeces of Painters'")

Some desperately poised against the orchestration. Here, in its entirety, is "Thinking Makes It So":

> *"Well, um, you know, something's neither good nor bad but thinking makes it so, I suppose, as Shakespeare said."*—Donald Rumsfeld

Less matter with more art, I say. Don't
retell the story of your brother and his
seven dogs minus one. How did it go?
The fussy clerk from the county office
called to inform your brother of his
need for a kennel license, so numerous
were the hounds roaming his property.

You first told me this story while we were looking down
            into a volcanic crater
    filled with a lake so blue the sky was ashamed of itself.

What, your brother asked, *is the limit?*
Seven, said the clerk, and your brother
called over his favorite hound, pulled
out his pistol, and shot the dog between
the eyes. He did this while the poor
clerk was still hanging on the line.
There, he said, *now I've got six.*

The favorite hound, his eyes on the master. The blue lake where once the mountain blew its top off. Counterarguments that ought to make us ashamed of ourselves.

We Don't Know We Don't Know is a brilliant book about the brutal limits of sympathy and imagination. Which is to say, it nurtures, brilliantly, the sympathy and imagination that might restore us. In "Augury," the poet recalls an ancient practice designed to expand the limits of knowledge by means of scrupulous reading: one thinks of the entrails of birds. But the poem suggests another way:

Catalogue of the sightless: the mole,
                 the olm, the horse
     that survived the fire. . . .
           If loss does not transform us. . . .
          If without form we
              are lost. . . .

If the bird turns and speaks to you in human words.

Which in these poems, it seems, miraculously, to do.

Linda Gregerson

We Don't Know We Don't Know

"*Reports that say that something hasn't happened are always interesting to me, because as we know, there are known knowns; there are things we know we know. We also know there are known unknowns; that is to say we know there are some things we do not know. But there are also unknown unknowns—the ones we don't know we don't know.*"
—Donald Rumsfeld, U.S. Secretary of Defense

"*As for all other living creatures, there is not one, but by a secret instinct of nature knoweth his own good, and wherto he is made able; some make use of their swift feet, others of their flight wings; some are strong of limne; others are apt to swim, and practise the same: man only knoweth nothing unlesse he be taught.*"
—Pliny the Elder (trans. Philemon Holland)

Known Knowns

Ancient Theories

A horse hair falls into the water and grows into an eel.
    Even Aristotle believed that frogs
                    formed from mud,
that mice sprouted like seedlings in the damp hay.

    I used to believe the world spoke
              in code. I lay awake
and tried to parse the flashes of the streetlight—
    obscured, revealed,
                obscured by the wind-sprung tree.
Stranded with you at the Ferris wheel's apogee
    I learned the physics
            of desire—fixed at the center,
it spins and goes nowhere.

    Pliny described eight-foot lobsters
           sunning themselves
on the banks of the Ganges. The cuckoo devouring
    its foster mother. Bees alighting
           on Plato's young lips.

In the Andes, a lake disappears overnight, sucked
    through cracks in the earth.
           How can I explain
the sunlight stippling your face in the early morning?

Why not believe that the eye throws its own light,
    that seeing illuminates
        the world?
        On the moon,
astronaut David Scott drops a hammer and a falcon feather,
    and we learn nothing
        we didn't already know.

Too Many, Too Few

"There's another way to phrase that and that is that the absence of evidence is not the evidence of absence. It is basically saying the same thing in a different way."—Donald Rumsfeld

There are too many finches, too few
        Darwins. Too many
                baroque Christs glooming
from their gilt frames, too few clouds
        gawking rails of light.

The wren doesn't stay behind
            to count each flake
        of snow filling
her abandoned nest, which isn't
            to say she doesn't
        consider it
during the taut respites between
            wing-beats.

I look out and I see too many
        people and too few, which is a different
way of saying
        the same thing, which is a way
of saying I'm tired
of saying the same thing, which is a way
        of saying I find no evidence
        of change, which is a way
of saying that even
        decline can be a kind of steadiness.

The archipelago's isles
        bunch up
        in the distance,

but this is a trick
        of perspective:
     the straits between
are miles across,

       and whatever
    land we settle on
is always windswept
        and wide.

"The order that Bees keepe in their worke"

"What display of human genius, in a word, shall we compare with the reasoning powers manifested by them?" —Pliny the Elder

1. Pulpit (West Ingraham, MA)

It is well-known that bees tend to swarm on Sundays, and often
a farmer must choose between losing his bees and attending worship.

> If my throat were   a jittery hive of voices that one day
> empties. If my tongue were the abandoned Jamestown settlement.
> If my mouth were the ruins   of Chichen Itza.

Those born in the cold do not learn to dance. When they speak,
no one listens. At first, only   a syllable mislaid
under the tongue, a word   lost in a canyon echo.

> The breath, as it leaves   the body, believes
> that one day it will   find a way back.

But they do not return. Their bodies   are found
on the grass, miles   from the hive, like discarded coins.

2. Leper's Window (Kloster Oesede, Germany)

Here we knelt by the outer wall and listened to the buzz
of the congregation, though through our hole we saw only
a sliver   of the sanctuary. When the priest raised
the host, a boy rang a bell and we pressed to the crack.

> The bee's eye comprises thousands of hexagons.
> The eye inscribes its pattern on the mind, and for this
> reason Plato loved the bee, its six legs and six-sided
> dreams. No bee ever thought to build a honeycomb
> of three- or five-sided chambers.

God was only ever as big as the hole we saw him through.

The omphalos stone, navel of the world,
was shaped like a beehive. The priestess
at Delphi was known as the Delphic Bee.

To say that we loved what we saw is not the same
as saying that we saw what we loved.

3. Ossuary (Sedlec, Czech Republic)

Pollen means, My breath into your mouth.
Wax means, Only for a little while.
Honey means, With your permission, oh lord.

For what festival have you hung these garlands
of skulls? What dance are we expected
to dance below a chandelier containing every
bone in the human body? Whose coat
of arms is this? A femur and coccyx stand
for a flaming branch, which stands
for the dominion of one people over another.
Bundles of ribs for golden sheaves. Half
a pelvis and a broken humerus arranged
in the shape of a raven, four metatarsals for its wing.
The bird is pecking at the empty
eye socket of a skull, which stands for a skull.

I wish I could say it reminded me of the grammar
of flight, the wind-stirred lexicon of flowers.
But it was so long ago, that first
hive: atoms buzzing in our jaws, man and woman
pocketed in their dark chambers, waiting.

What Is Not Inside the Head-Sized Box

Who can say where Petrarch's skull has gone, where God
    hid the body of Moses? The squirrel doesn't
                                  remember
every cache of food; he plays the odds just like any of us.

    The rebel buries mines in his own
                              fields, knowing
that if he survives the war, his plow may one day
    open a white-hot seam
                  in the earth.

In the pantry, the naked potato sprouts despite its lack
    of dirt. The fox promises
            a mountain of gold if you
can tell him how many stones will fit in an empty sack.

    The Buddha carried a small
            lacquered box with him
on his travels. Though his disciples begged and begged,
    he refused, even on his deathbed,
                to reveal its contents.
A starving bear will flip over the same boulder again
    and again, expecting each time
            to find something to eat.

The empty mind has room enough for only one thought.
    My dog stares so lovingly
            at my empty hand. When asked
if he could see anything inside Tutankhamen's tomb,
    Howard Carter turned and said "Yes,
                wonderful things."

Things Will Not

"Things will not be necessarily continuous. The fact that they are something other than perfectly continuous ought not to be characterized as a pause. There will be some things that people will see. There will be some things that people won't see. And life goes on."—Donald Rumsfeld

One day you turn   your head: swallows
have built a nest of straw and mud, glued it
to the window pane with their own spit,
where before there was awning, gutter,
branch, a trapezoid of sky and
            How does anything happen?

(To say that the heart rests between
beats says nothing of its tirelessness.)

In the other room someone   you love
plays scales on the piano. Now she's found
one wrong note, a loose   string,
      and plays it over and over.

In diorama, in leaps: the eggs appear,
the chicks appear (first three, then
                  without explanation
only two), then the empty, shit-covered
nest you must knock off with a broom.
      (Swing carefully, so as not
            to break the glass.)

      Here comes the music, now, the song
stepping around the one note it can't make.

To say that light transfigures a window
says nothing   about the view.

To say   even that a word
is a house of wattle and daub obstructing
a view is insufficient. (How can any word
          be sufficient?)

The heart plays legato, or it plays staccato,
but it is the same song, tireless   and raw
          and dull as any love that has forgotten itself.

You watch swallows weaving in the gaps
between the trees until
                              it is too dark outside
to see even the last outline of a branch.
But to say you see nothing
                    is not to say much of anything.

Snapshot from Turkey

In Bodrum we saw
a boy spinning a top
in the street. While we
watched from a cafe,
he kept the top going
for an hour by flailing
it with a little whip.
We asked him why
he enjoyed the game
so much, and he said:
[   ].
We later translated
this to mean: The whip
makes a pleasing
sound when it strikes.

"Whether the World be finite, and but one"

"as who would say, a man could take the measure just of any third thing,
who knoweth not his owne: or the minde of man see those things, which
the very World itselfe may not receive."—Pliny the Elder

Here is the painting of the edge
                    of the world. It is not
          what you expect. The barn, its door agape,
     its interior implosive with darkness. The split
rail fence, the hand-painted sign
                    warning away the curious.
          The lettering is too small to read from this
     distance, and we will only ever see
the edge of the world from this distance,
                              the velvet cordon
          bumping at our waists,
the museum guard coughing.

     Someone says,
                 This world is overrated.
     Someone says,
                 Beyond this earth is another.
     Someone says,
                 The artist died of syphilis.
     Someone says,
                 He was struck blind.
     By stroke, says one.
                 By god, says another.

They all agree the painting is beautiful.
                         In the foreground,
             a slouching sheaf of wheat. In its center,
          says the docent, the grain has begun
to rot. Where is the farmer? someone calls out.

Curvilinear roof, asymptotic sky. The title
                    is cut
            into the paint with a palette knife. *Here,*
    it says, *Then nothing*. What did you expect?

The Collapse of a Twenty-Story Bamboo Construction Scaffold Caught on Home Video— Hong Kong, September 12, 2002

Until you play the tape backward,
you do not see the body: live and leaping
into the reassembling wreckage.

List of Things We Know

40% of all
births are
accidental.
10% of all
accidents
are births.
Kindness
is correlated
to detached
earlobes,
a damaged
amygdala,
a person's
credit rating,
but in all cases
the direction
of causality
is unclear.
Chances are,
your husband
is lying to
you. Most
substances
contract when
frozen, but
ice expands;
for this reason,
the oceans do
not freeze,
and we can
go on living.
If you see
a ripped pair
of underwear

in the bushes
by the bus
depot, assume
the worst.
Pollen leaps
from flower
to bee, but
this is only
static electricity,
not the work
of affection.
We've proven
experimentally
that the mouse
feels fear (we
haven't yet
devised a test
to determine
if he feels joy).

Lacuna, Triptych of the Battle

—Artist unknown, ca. 1230 AD

First Panel

A confusion of soldiers—the guide counts
for us ten helmeted heads but twenty-five
boots—cramped below the castle wall.
Are they mustering for a surge or balking
just beyond the archers' reach?

Second Panel

Ripped away, only a skirt of paint hemming
top and bottom, forty-seven boots kissing,
toe-to-toe. At the top, a ribbon of sky, a broken
spearhead hangs loose in the air, like an iron
falcon folded to drop. So rare, says the guide,
for motion to be conveyed this way.

Third Panel

An army victorious, but high on the flagpole
its standard has been pried away for its gold
enamel, so who can say which army
it is, invader or defender? The guide smiles,
points to the missing triangle. This theft
too, he says, is hundreds of years
old. This theft too is part of history.

Vermeer's *Woman Reading a Letter*
at an Open Window

> *"If I said yes, that would then suggest that that might be the only place*
> *where it might be done which would not be accurate, necessarily accurate.*
> *It might also not be inaccurate, but I'm disinclined to mislead anyone."*
> —Donald Rumsfeld

I think it must always be the same
light in Vermeer's paintings, here
a girl laughing at an officer's joke,
a geographer pausing to look up
from his maps, a woman practicing
the lute, her fingers curled around
the neck, its body pressed to hers.

The light always falls from the left.
The window may have many panes
or few, the room bigger or smaller.

Vermeer's light fools you. It comes
from a world outside the window,
outside the painting, a world greater
than the sleepy canals of Delft.

Here is my desk, the window to my
left, but where is the light Vermeer
saw? I look outside and see a hawk
swooping for rabbits in the yard,
the municipal mowers trimming
the median grass, a parking lot
that fills and empties like a lung.

My wife looks at these paintings
and says that many of the women

are pregnant. *Here,* she points,
the woman's waist, how the dress
is unbelted? I grow impatient.
What about the light? I say. I want
to say that Vermeer has painted
these men and women only to give
the light something to fall against.
Instead we argue for hours about
whether the women are pregnant.

I want to believe in a room filled
with Vermeer's light, the world
outside the room that glows so
warmly, the people who spend
all day gathered by the window.

When my wife and I reconcile,
we're lying together on the couch
late at night. The blinds are drawn.
The only light comes from the TV.

Here is a woman reading a letter
by an open window. She's nearing
the letter's end—some news, good
or bad, from the impossible world
outside. Here are her small hands,
the curled paper, an overturned
bowl of fruit, the same light falling.

Known Unknowns

Will There Be More Than One "Questioner"?

—CIA *Human Resource Exploitation Training Manual* (1983)

Will the cell window look out onto a hem of mountains? An alley of hard-
    packed dirt? A seam of razor wire?
Will the "questioning" take place in the cell or at another location?
In the location where the "questioning" will take place, have provisions
    been made for restraints?
Will you know the crime of which he is accused before you begin the
    "questioning"?
Have provisions been made for surveillance?
Have provisions been made for refreshments?
Will there be light?
Will there be music?
During the day will all light be shut out?
Will you read the name on his dossier before entering the cell?
Before the "questioning" begins, will you offer tea scented with rose
    water?
Will you take his hand in yours?
Will you send for ████████████████?
After the first day of "questioning," will you sit on the breezy veranda
    and read the confiscated letters from his wife?
Will it concern you that the detention center has a veranda in the first
    place, that from the nearest road, it looks like a rich man's estate,
    sprawl of tan buildings collared by a tender lawn?
For this reason, will you give him your real name even though to do so is
    forbidden?
Will you have an unconscious man dragged past the open door at a
    predetermined time?
Will you say, Excuse me, and then rise to shut the door?
Will you remember that the anticipation of pain is more acute than pain
    itself?
Will his wife send the same letter to every embassy, every week, for
    months?

What kind of music will be playing at night?
Will the unconscious man be missing his nose?
Will you ask questions you know are beyond his knowledge?
Will you ask questions that have no answers?
Will he say, No more for today, please?
Will you listen?
In the letters his wife sends, will she have left a blank space exactly the
    length of the words *Where are you*?
Will there be a window at all?
Will you show him your pistol just once?
Will you ask him what he did before the war?
Will a bucket in the corner continue to catch the drip of water?
Will he say, I was a farmer?
Will he say, I salvaged scrap metal?
Will he say, I was a faith healer who traveled in a covered wagon?
Will he say, I was a thief?
Will he say, I was an interrogator?
Will he say, I was a weaver?
Will you admit you've never understood the mechanics of the loom, how
    the shuttle racks back and forth and a pattern emerges?
Will he say, The loom has been more essential to the development of
    civilization than has the printing press or the cotton gin?
Will he say, I was a scribe when the centurions crucified your god?
Will you ask, How could you sit by and do nothing?
Will he say, It was my job to record such things, not to intercede?
Will you ask the stenographer to strike his last statement from the record?
Will there be a stenographer?
Will there be any record of what you've done, what you plan to do?
After many weeks, during a lull in the "questioning," will you speak of the
    first time your fingers grazed the inside of your wife's thigh?
Will he nod and say, Yes, I remember too, the smell of my own wife's hair
    on my face in the morning?
Will you ask him how he can remember anything?
Will he admit that more than once he has tried drowning himself in that
    bucket of dripped-down water?
Will you say, I know, we watch you day and night?

Will he ask, How could you sit by and do nothing?

Will you say, We thought you were praying?

Will you say, Even to witness an atrocity is a kind of courage?

Will you say, The remedy is worse than the disease?

Will you say, I misspoke, we see nothing?

Will you say, Such things are not up to me?

Will he say, After I failed, I had to wait ten years for the bucket to fill so I
    could try again?

Will you say, It was a hundred years?

Will he say, ▮▮▮▮▮▮▮▮▮▮▮▮▮▮▮▮▮▮▮▮▮?

Will you ask, How are such wonders possible?

Will he say, The shuttle of the loom whispers as it makes its pass over the
    threads?

Will there be a translator?

At night will you rub the bumpy skin of his passport between your
    fingers?

Will you think of him while you eat dark honey smeared on dark bread in
    a cafe?

Will you sign the order?

Will you say, If it were up to me...?

The night before, will you keep him awake with unscripted questions?

Will you ask, When you were a healer, would you heal anyone? When you
    were a scribe, what did you omit? When you were a thief, did you
    steal from yourself?

Will he say, Questions in sufficient quantity are a kind of answer?

Will you ask, Like the drops falling into the bucket?

And will he say, No, not like that at all?

Many months later, will you recognize his wife buying loose tea and
    oranges from the market?

Will you take her picture from his dossier and carry it in your inside breast
    pocket?

Will you have her followed?

Will you sit in your car outside her house, which was once their house?

Will the house be made of marble? Sheets of corrugated tin? Bones and
    hide?

Will you approach her at the gate one morning and touch her arm, though
    to do so is forbidden, even for you?
Will you risk everything to say, He is alive, he is alive?
Will it be true?
Will she call out for help?
Will the bucket in the corner overflow?
Will you say, The anticipation of death is worse than death itself?
Will you say this to no one in particular?
Will you go to his cell, sit in the chair he sat in, and imagine your own
    face staring at you across the pocked table, your open mouth a hole
    that water drips through day and night?
Will there be light?
Will there be ~~consolation~~?
Will there be more than one "questioner"?
Will there be more than one "question"?
Will the loom hold taut the warp as the weft passes through?
Will a pattern emerge?
Will there be a witness to all we have said and done?

Unknown Unknowns

Potemkin Village: Ars Poetica

Verisimilitude requires
a homeless man's feet
protruding from a dark
vestibule. Empty huts
will fool no one. If
I say do not look there,
you will look more
closely, so I say, look,
for God's sake look.
The men and women:
papier-mâché flesh,
one bare bulb burning
in each ribcage. From
this distance, light can
resemble life. See
how they wave to you.

"Of the Parrat and other birds that can speake"

"It is for certain knowne that they have died for very anger and griefe that they could not learn to pronounce some hard words."—Pliny the Elder

When you buy the bird for your mother
you hope it will talk to her. But weeks pass
before it does anything except pluck the bars
with its beak. Then one day it says, "infect."

Your mother tells you this on the phone,
and you drive over, find the frozen meals
you bought for her last week sweating
on the countertop. "In fact," she says

in answer to your question, "I *have* been
eating," and it's as you point to the empty
trash can, the spotless dishes, that you
realize the bird is only saying, "in fact,"

that this is now the preamble to all
of your mother's lies. "In fact," she says,
"I have been paying the bills," and you
believe her until you find a cache

of unopened envelopes in the freezer.
More things are showing up where
they shouldn't. Looking out the back
window one evening you see craters

in her yard. While she's watching TV,
you go out with a trowel and excavate
picture frames, flatware that looks like
the silver bones of some exquisite

animal. You worry when you arrive
one day and see the open, empty cage
that you will find the bird dead, stuffed
in an oven mitt and left in a drawer,

but you find it sitting on her shoulder
in the kitchen. "In fact," she says,
"he learned to open the cage himself."
The bird learns new words. You learn

which lies you can ignore. The stroke
that kills her gives no warning, not—
the doctor assures you—that anyone
can predict such things. When you

drive home that night with the cage
belted into the passenger seat, the bird
makes a sound that is not a word
but that you immediately recognize

as the sound of your mother's phone
ringing, and you know it is the sound
of you calling her again and again,
the sound of her not answering.

[   ]

Eve refuses to name the animals.
Adam, cross-legged atop his hillock,
points like a retarded child at each
creature as it presents itself to him.
Camel, he says. Water buffalo. Ant.
Eve dreams of a time when sound
was only sound. Love is a ratchet,
Adam says to her that night. You
cinch it tighter every day. Each new
name is like a boulder grinding
into place over the mouth of her cave.
She says   , and he looks
at her. Pity: another word thanks
to him. Since when, she wonders,
is a cave like a mouth? Since when
is any thing like anything else?
And look what she's stuck with:
stones circling the fire pit, kindling,
flint. They grow smaller each time
she repeats their names. Only a stone,
only a branch (a dead branch, she
now knows), only a word, only me.

Thinking Makes It So

"Well, um, you know, something's neither good nor bad but thinking makes it so, I suppose, as Shakespeare said."—Donald Rumsfeld

Less matter with more art, I say. Don't
retell the story of your brother and his
seven dogs minus one. How did it go?
The fussy clerk from the county office
called to inform your brother of his
need for a kennel license, so numerous
were the hounds roaming his property.

    You first told me this story while we were looking down
            into a volcanic crater
      filled with a lake so blue the sky was ashamed of itself.

What, your brother asked, *is the limit?*
Seven, said the clerk, and your brother
called over his favorite hound, pulled
out his pistol, and shot the dog between
the eyes. He did this while the poor
clerk was still hanging on the line.
There, he said, *now I've got six.*

Augury

Go on eating around the apple's bruises. The first
    cardinal weaving the fence line a red
                miracle. If rain
drumming the bedroom eaves does not wake you.

    Each face sunk in a nimbus of foam.
                Go on cutting
the eyes out of the potato. In a fire, brooding storks
    will be consumed with the nest
                rather than abandon it.

If [   ] is forgotten. Those first days after the surgery,
    you wondered if sight would
                return. The gauze a caul.
Go on counting the lisping ticks of the second hand.

    The anemones in the pale cave
                gasping. If the drunk
in the stairwell finishes the song he's singing. Clouds
    lather. If the phone rings and rings and
                rings and rings.
If the cricket dies making the same desperate music.

    Catalogue of the sightless: the mole,
                the olm, the horse
that survived the fire. If the two-headed calf starves.
    When no one was home you rose
                and felt your way
to the kitchen. If loss does not transform us. A glass
    of water. If without form we
                are lost. If years go by.

Go on sanding the burl of memory. From the brush
    a salvo of sparrows. If the wildfire
                  crosses the river.
If the bird turns and speaks to you in human words.

"Of Swine, and their nature"

"There is not the flesh of any other living creature, that yeeldeth more store of dishes to the maintenance of gluttonie, than this."

—Pliny the Elder

Lean over the stile
and put your hand
to their flesh, valves
of their beating hearts
so like our own and yet.
Year round, trucks back
up to the chute and pull
away, gasp of pneumatic
brakes. The distance
between us and them
infinitely divisible.
The signs call this
place a confinement.
A crow types his lines
of cuneiform across
the snowy yard, and you
think only of apples,
minimum monthly
payments as paralyzing
as Zeno's paradox,
rhomboid barn frames
you pass on the drive
to work, siding stripped
for craft-fair scrap. Last
weekend, you wandered
into the swale behind
your house and caught
two teenagers hammering
railroad spikes into a tree.

Every morning, your wife
dips her finger in camphor
and draws two O's
on your nostrils. You can
think only of apples,
the indivisible sweetness
of memory, days when
the wind shifts and you can
forget. Every so often
a boar stops on the ramp,
trembling, calligraphy
of its breath written
for a moment in the air,
then drops dead of heart
failure. After the teenagers
ran away you went back
to the house and cooked
dinner. The wind shifts
again and you remember.
The soft meat you hold
in your hand for a minute
above the singing skillet,
the transmutation of flesh
to flesh, life to life. A gilt
may eat her young if not
properly supervised. They
call this savaging. You
smell it even in your sleep.
You break off a flake
of paint from the house
and crush it between your
fingers. Even the dust stinks
of excrement, or maybe it is
your own skin. At least,
your friends say, you don't
work at the slaughterhouse.

The Prophecies of Paracelsus

That twig of light, that branch, that
                              fork, that form.
                 Beyond that, a city. A horse drowning in
      a river, and beyond that, a city. Wildfire, and beyond that,
a city. God, a slippery thing,
                    an eel, is twined
          from our hands. That rainy hum is
     the wharf, is the light that etches a bridge
                         between pronouns, the bottle
of amber formaldehyde, the infant
                              orangutan, the wing
           of a gull stitched to its scapula. Here is a river
       drowning in a horse's dark eye. Devitalized, humming, rainy,
the feather of this gull, this small
                    spill of light,
          the written thing that glues each hill
     to the earth, that follows a pull with its wobbly needle. God is
a drowned horse fifty hands at the shoulder. To write what
                         convinces with
          the impossible whisper. After that,
     a city. They call this floating thing an angel and hurry you out
          of the tent. A bear eating its own paws, and after
                    this, a city. A window full
of smoke, and after this, a city. A meter to measure
                                        day and time.
Adapted for that purpose by the God of our hands.

Your Family's Farm, Empty

"Buildings can't want."—Donald Rumsfeld

Neither does the ax regret each tree it has bitten,
    though it leans against the shed
like a drunk locked out of his own house.

The tractor doesn't moon
over the physique of its youth.
The dry birdbath makes no plans
for the future.

    What can the barn recall of the day
you climbed the ladder into its loft and found

a pair of buzzard chicks
    skulking among the hay bales?
Your grandfather shot them with a pistol

and kicked them out of the haymow for you
to carry to the ditch beyond the field.

Does the barn remember those shots
    exploding inside it like a burst neuron?
    The weight of those bodies thudding to earth?

Can the field remember your feet crossing it, the air
    heavy with crickets?
Does the ditch remember the bones the coyotes
    gnawed and scattered?

You stand here, where the walnut tree was felled,
    one foot on the smooth disc of the stump.

The grass makes no demands on your soul.
The cow paths are as forgetful as the rain.

If it is possible,
        the kennel
grown over with morning glories
is less than indifferent to silence.

What We Know of Death by Drowning

1. Josef Mengele Drowns While Swimming at a Beach in Brazil, 1979

His name then: Wolfgang Gerhard.
How easy, slipping on another man's
      skin. Another country, too,

its sun's heat and light
as insistent as a pair
of forceps.

His pants, left crumpled
on the beach, forged papers
and a few hard candies in the pocket.

Where the water
      was shallow, he could look
      down and see

his shadow passing over
the pale sand, a wobbly twin,

      matching him
stroke for stroke for stroke.

2. Li Po Drowns Trying to Embrace the Reflection of the Moon in the Yangtze, 762

The moon is no drinker of wine, so I must
compensate. Surely you've heard

the crows and nightingales
egging me on? The day has dispersed
from the courtyards like a gang
      of sparrows, and nothing

is left of the world that is not
pecked-over, hard and dark
     as the dream of an apple seed.

The young men laugh
at an old man drinking
alone, but here

are my companions:
     my shadow, as loyal
     and thin as a starved dog,

and the moon, his whole face
     wrinkling with laughter.

3. Bob, the Circus Seal, Drowns Himself in His Tank in Galveston, 1911

By then his teeth had rotted out,
     and he often turned to his owner
with his mouth open as if about

to speak, a ruined smell
jetting from inside.

He had already attempted it,

     three days before,
but his owner dove in and pulled him up
onto the slimy planks. His circus show days

were long gone. Sure, some afternoons
a kid might walk by
     and see the scabby painting

on the side of the building: the hoop,
the pedestal, the ghost
of a man in a top hat,

the striped ball now like a clot
of pus streaked
with blood, hovering

over the sleek, dark head.

4. Natalie Wood Drowns under Mysterious Circumstances near Santa Catalina Island, 1981

Let me tell you: death
        is a long silk glove
dropped to the floor.

It doesn't remember the heft
of the arm, the fingers
        dancing.

That limb is gone, and nothing
will hold its shape again.

You twirl your pastel skirt. You watch
two cars
race toward the cliff,
        and there is nothing

you can do. So many lives
        you've entered
like a room: swooned,

held the prop pistol
to your own face, sang
for the back row.

But was it your voice?

What was that name
you were born into?
        Natalia Nikolaevna Zakharenko?
What happened to her?

        Was she the one
taken, her family butchered, living
another life
among an enemy people?

Was it the morning
when she stopped scanning
the horizon for rescuers
        that she turned into you?

5. Hippasus of Metapontum Is Drowned at Sea for the Heresy of Discovering Irrational Numbers, ca. 500 BCE

His fellow Pythagoreans had already built
a shrine to his memory
        and placed it where

he passed by every day, but he did not take
        the hint. It was on the ship
that they seized him.

God was an integer, firm
as an unripe apricot.
        But weren't there streets
        in the city that wound forever
into the minute darkness?

Weren't there dreams where he met
himself again and again,
without ever seeming to wake?

The sea is incommensurable.
    Each lungful of air
        kept dividing itself, even as the boat

became a decimal point on the far horizon.

6. Bennie Wint, 20 Years after Faking His Drowning Death, Is Discovered Alive, 2009

In the first years after I disappeared, I read
every report of drowning: children,

mostly boys,
mostly in their bathtubs,
mostly accidents.

Old men whose lungs filled with fluid
        while they sat in their armchairs.

Fishermen. Swimmers. Immigrants
crowded onto rafts. Some men,
    their throats seize up,
    and they die without

ever swallowing a drop,
as if they never left the shore.

    Some nights I dreamed
what never happened: I held my drowning

in my palm like a giant pearl.
    Some days, standing behind
the cash register of my new life,

I felt my lungs flatten out like a pair
of discarded socks. Did I ever think

of the woman I left on the shore
        as I kicked out
past the last of the breakers?

I won't say.

Here it was: I might have drowned
trying to pretend to. I had to swim
so far out, then mark

a different beach
and swim back

a different man, without knowing
if his strength was enough
        to carry me to shore.

Either Or

You haven't heard
from your father
in six months
and you can't
bring yourself
to call. In Bengal,
farmers wore
masks on the backs
of their heads
to ward off tigers,
who, one supposes,
wouldn't attack
a man who was
watching. If I don't
call, you thought,
nothing is wrong.
Each possibility is
a cavern eaten
out of limestone
by water. Naming
everything is a way
of naming nothing.
His family dropped
away like cicada
husks swept off
tree trunks by rain.
One brother, heart
attack. His father's
two feet taken
by diabetes, then

his father by stroke.
In a tornado, leave
your windows ajar.
A doorway for
an earthquake.
In a lightning storm,
do not pick up
the phone. Learn
to see out the back
of your head. His
youngest brother,
weeks dead before
discovery: the couch
where he died,
face down, shadow
of rotted flesh
stained into fabric,
ghost of a face.
Imagination kills
the living just
as easily as it brings
back the dead.
In Turkey, they hang
the nazar—teardrop
of blue glass—
on lintels, above
beds, from the rearview
mirror. To ward
off evil, they say.

Harry Harlow in the Pit of Despair

It's easy enough to be thankful for the robin's dappled
    egg, the crepuscular rays gouging
                through the clouds.
Even the caged monkey can blow kisses at its captors.

    Why don't the crow's feet freeze
              to the snowy branch?
Why doesn't the worm in his hole die of shame? Let us
    go on loving each other as if
              none of this matters.

All winter the sun lolls low across the horizon. What
    drives us out with a broom
              each morning to knock
the fangs of ice from the eaves of our lover's house?

    Our vice is born in a folk tale:
              a fox by the roadside
feigning a lame foot, a scorpion asleep in a traveler's
    boot, a fish singing
              to the fisherman's wife.
Why should it surprise us that affection can limp past
    the gates of cruelty? Should it
              astonish that we walk
so slowly when we return to an empty house?

Yes, the lamprey lives and dies
              by its lingering kiss.
Harry, after the long months of stumbling darkness,
    what will emerge to greet
              us with outstretched arms?

"Of Dogges"

"They alone know their owne names."—Pliny the Elder

This goes on for years, a grey dog trotting
        down the gravel road every morning, your house
    the same house it has been since it became a house.

You go about your life. The tall grass nods
        at everything and nothing. The windows have no
    opinion. A hand closes over something, the light

falls a certain way on the ground. Each evening,
        the dog returns, covered in dust, paws whispering
    on the gravel as he passes your house, a scrap

of dusk roaming toward home. This is nothing
        new, but tonight something has changed: where
    is the white circle around the eye, the notched

ear, that old wound you've come to recognize?
        The dog seems younger than you remember,
    and for the first time you wonder

where he goes. Far off, clouds equivocate.
        Rain glances at the earth then turns away.
    Already you have begun to forget

the dog. The same dinner you cook every night,
        steam fogging your eyes as you shake
    out the same pasta. The same story

on the news. The same aching wrists, the same
        snug belt. The same long drive to and from work,
    the inert nipple of the radio dial between

your thumb and finger, the miles of road where
	you can't pick up anything clearly. Then one day
	there is a car, like any other car, stirring

a plume of dust along the road, and there
	is the dog, dead in the road. Or not dead
	yet, but dying. You put it in your truck

and drive up the road, past the last of the houses
	that you know. You find a house you've never
	seen before, though it is like any other house.

You recognize it because the yard is full
	of grey dogs. They are not the same dog,
	and you wonder how many you've watched

walk by your window. The owner comes out, looks
	in the back of your truck, shrugs. The other
	dogs crowd around you, and you ask about

the dog with the notched ear. What was its name?
	Where did it go? The other dogs look at you.
	Some of them are missing legs. One is blind.

The light decants from horizon to road. You drive
	past your own house. You see a pumpkin patch full
	of pumpkins, their many variations:

cockeyed lobes, mottled, smooth, shapes that imply
	imperceptible slopes of earth, drops of rain wetting
	tender shoots, a month of drought, a dog

running past. You think of the room you grew up in,
	in another house, honeyed light playing on the wall.
	That dog? the man said. That dog died years ago.

_____, for Which There Is No Translation

Traduttore, traditore (Proverb)

_____, by which the islanders mean an empty boat
                             alone on the water,
one's only boat, which has drifted off, too far out
for even the strongest swimmer
                             to reach, beyond
saving, which is to say hopeless, but visibly so, and thus
a reminder of how seeing something
                             is not the same as possessing it.

_____, by which travelers mean falling asleep on a train
and waking hours later to discover that the other passengers
                             have all been replaced
by new travelers, that even the agent who punched your ticket
                             is gone, has ended
his shift at some earlier station, and your heart feels
like a pair of couplers holding two freight cars
                             together in a long turn.

_____, by which the bereaved mean the memory of walking
into the house and seeing some small object
                             askew: half-flayed orange
left on the table, cup of tea gone cold, dog-eared magazine
                             pages flailing in the breeze.

_____, by which I mean an ice storm, one that glazes
each leaf of the backyard maple—creating, after
                             the real leaves have dropped
away, ice replicas, each xylem and phloem preserved
                             as if cut into
glass, though of course they are not really leaves, no matter how
                             they dazzle you.

52

Unknown Knowns

"The Decay of ancient knowledge"

"considering that by such trade and entercourse, all things heretofore unkowne, might have come to light."—Pliny the Elder

To cure a child of rickets, split a living
ash tree down its length and pass
the child through
  (naked, headfirst, three times).
Seal the two halves of the tree back up
and bind them with loam and black
thread. If the tree heals, so will the child.
  (The child must also be washed
  for three mornings in the dew
    of the chosen tree.)

Two men
  (no, women)
    must pass the child through.
The first must say, "The Lord receives,"
and the second say, "The Lord gives."

This is how you ensure a happy marriage:
This is how you keep the engine running:

A jackdaw or swallow that flies down
the chimney must be
    killed. If it is allowed
to leave the house by a window or door,
a member of the family will

This is how, when your mother tells
you she's going in for biopsy, to make
the growth benign:

Burn a fire and in the morning examine
the ashes for footprints, the image of a ring,
the likeness of a car, a bed, a horse, a

This is how you keep from thinking of
the one thought you're thinking:

Say your own name backwards three
(no four) times and turn around (keep
your eyes shut).

The unborn child must be called *pot lid*
or *tea kettle* until you hear its voice.

Carry a live bat around the house three
times, then nail it upside down outside
the window. This will ensure

If your mother calls you at 6 A.M. while
she eats her breakfast (do not eat after
7), this is how you can calm your voice:

This is how you say *Good luck* and mean

An egg laid on Sunday can be placed
on the roof to ward off fire and lightning.

If you put a stillborn child in an open
grave, the man who is buried there will
have a ticket straight to heaven.

Never sleep with your feet toward the door.

Do not sneeze while making a bed.

Step on a beetle, and it will rain. Bury it
alive in the earth for good weather. Put it
in your mouth and your loved ones will

When you see a dead bird lying in the road
you must spit on it.

If a rooster crows in the night, you must
go and feel his feet.

When a woman is in labor, all the locks
in the house must be undone, windows
and doors must be left ajar. This will
not prevent death but will quicken
the escape of the spirit if

If the ash tree remedy fails, bring the child
to a third
        (no, seventh)
                        generation blacksmith.
The child must first be bathed
in the water trough, then laid on the anvil.
Each of the smith's tool's must be passed
over the body, and each time one must
inquire what the tool is used for (no one
must answer). Then the blacksmith must
raise his hammer and bring it down (gently)
three times (four) on the child's body.
                If a fee is given
or even asked for, the cure will not

If the phone rings, this is how you answer:
This is how you say, How did it go?

By Way of Explanation, No Jug without Kiln

If, then. If I could speak, then.

    Here are the conditions:
no honeycomb
without servility,
no grief without
the whale's fist-
sized eye, no
ambulance without
stone scraping
stone, no gravity
without landfill, no
Appalachia without
oxygen, no oppression
without metallurgy,
no lettuce without
the possum caught
hissing in the daylight,
no hospital gurney
wheel without opera,
no orchard smell
without acceleration,
no appetite without
mine cave-ins,
no shopping carts
without miscarriage,
no alchemy without
sleight-of-hand, no
leopard teeth without
miracles, no leprosy
without excuses, no
hovering hawk without
a woman's refusal to

speak, no lamp oil
without pyramids
eaten by jungle, no
jug without kiln

    Addendum: I will sit here all day; that much
    is settled. That much you can depend on.

Those are the conditions, but you don't have to
say anything to me about it yet.

What Caravaggio's *Narcissus* Does Not See in the Water

The inverted heron. The spurious clouds gliding
    like gauzy parallelograms. In my
            favorite self-portrait,
I stare at my own reflection in the windshield.

    The finger that points only
          at itself. Your phone call
that led us to you, jumbled limbs, a delta of vomit
    spreading through
          the carpet. Years of this.
Hands, a square of naked flank, the ink dark eye.
    The first human speech, perfumed
          smoke rising
over a fire. The first words soft, stinging, like sea mist.

    When you live among such
          abundance, it's easy
to believe there are more shoes than feet in the world.
    Wherever the heron flies,
          it is always leaving.

On the seafloor, there are worms that can feed
    on the carcass of a whale
          for decades. Their children
drift in the dark currents, pale motes of hunger.

You're Going to Be Told

"I mean, you're going to be told lots of things. You get told things every day that don't happen. It doesn't seem to bother people. . . . The world thinks all these thing happen. They never happened."—Donald Rumsfeld

You never had a brother. Your family:
a crackpot conspiracy theory, your mother's
death from blood poisoning staged
on a Hollywood back lot. If you squint
at the memory, you can see the boom mike
dipping into the top of the frame,
the cardboard set wilting in the stage lights.
The man playing your father can't
remember his lines. He says, I forgot
her purse. We're out of leftovers, buy
yourself some burgers on the way home.
The money he gives you is just scraps
of newspaper dyed green. The brother
you never had drives the car, his face
fuzzed out like some obscene gesture.
He drives the car around the hospital
three times, and the building is only
a facade propped up by two-by-fours,
stuntmen in chaps and black Stetsons
perched on the roof. You make guns
with your hands and shoot them off,
and they sail down to the pavement
to the tune of a slide whistle. The brother
you never had giggles. He opens his
mouth and canned applause comes out.
He keeps driving around the hospital
in wider and wider circles, until you
are orbiting the earth. He looks out
the window and says, Death is the only

man-made object visible from space.
You say, None of this ever happened,
but even as you say it you can't help
looking down into that small room
where your mother is dying in the middle
of the camera crew's cigarette break.

Homeless in the Land of Aphorism

Vultures don't go   straight to the dead
but circle   for hours. Their patience is a hole

in the bottom of everything we don't know.
Let's face it: Yawning and   bombs are just

different   replacements for paradise.
The bat squeaks the same   question

into the dark all   night. There's nothing
left   to compare his disappointment to.

Think of all the beautiful Bigfoots striding
forever into   the forest of our unknowing.

Think of scribbles of light   left behind
by UFOs, ball   lightning, swamp gas.

Try not to think   of insensible columns
of black smoke rising over   the desert.

If the heart is a cracked   hornet's nest, then
the brain   is a jar of nails. Or is it the other

way around?   Somewhere, catfish are spawning
in the trunk of a submerged car   and couldn't

care less whether we   live or die.

As You Know

As you know, the human head is the most
    commonly stolen body part.
As you know, honey does not spoil, and for this
    reason it was used to embalm
        the bodies of kings.
As you know, dogs were also convicted
    of witchcraft and burned at the stake.
        So were chickens, fish, and a few trees.
As you know, some worms, if
    sufficiently starved, will eat
        their own bodies.
As you know, during the Cat Festival in Ypres,
    effigies of cats are thrown from a belfry tower
        (live cats were thrown until 1817).
        Revelers, dressed as cats and witches,
            dance in the street.
        As you know, this is the only event of interest
        ever to occur in Ypres.
As you know, an amputee may feel
    his missing limb moving
        of its own accord.
As you know, the word *gift* in German
    means *poison.*
As you know, a crow, finding three torn
    pieces of candy wrapper in the parking lot,
        will inspect each piece only once and then fly
            away. As you know,
        a seagull will return again and again to each scrap,
            always expecting to find the missing food.
As you know, at over 300 years old the Endicott Pear Tree
    in Danvers, Massachusetts is the oldest fruit-bearing tree
        in North America. It has survived four hurricanes
            and grew back when vandals cut off its trunk six feet
            above the ground.
        As you know, its pears are said to lack sweetness.

"The resemblance that Apes have to men"

"the sole of their foot is answerable to the palm of their hand."

—Pliny the Elder

The headlight is answerable to the car-struck coyote limping into the trees.
The kiln is answerable to the cathedral. A fence to the deer leaping over it.

Once the corpus callosum has been	severed,
the subject can no longer identify	an object
presented in the left visual field.	The right hand
will truly be ignorant of the left.	The military
is exploring practical applications	of the procedure.

The abandoned subway tunnel is answerable to a wildfire crossing a river.
The jet contrail to the horse's broken leg. The kidney, removed, to hail.

Thirty days	of isolation is enough
to ruin them.	The isolates
will reject	their young. (The less
said of the method	of insemination
the better.) One	new mother held
her infant's head	against the floor
and gnawed off	his fingers.

The greenness of grass to the abandoned pit mine over which it has grown.
The word *mine* to the flap of skin that covers the shark's eye when it strikes.

Tell me again of our	likeness. Tell me
again who	I am answerable to.

Coal is answerable to memory. Memory to a ratchet's pawl. My palm
to yours. Our extinction to a lever long enough to move the world.

A History of the Question Mark

"In reading, an interrogation generally requires a longer stop than a period; because an answer is either returned or implied; and consequently a proper interval of silence is necessary."
                    —Joseph Robertson, *An Essay on Punctuation* (1785)

The question mark as gaff hook plunged
into the sturgeon's gills, so much caviar

spilling out like a tangle of ellipses.
The question mark as crop circle, as embryo,

as single hair curled in an evidence bag,
as crescent of rust on an empty bucket.

The question mark as the moth's spiraled
proboscis as it unfurls to reach a flower.

A certain Sumerian pictogram: some say
an ox goad. Some say the secret name

of Enlil, god of wind, breath, and open space.
The question mark as heartworm looped

around the fist of the heart, as decades-old
knife wound, as beckoning finger, as lariat.

God said to Ezekiel, Mortal, eat this scroll.
When the prophet had finished, a black curl

of ink trailed from the corner of his mouth,
a single droplet dotting his throat.

The question mark as a child's ear
taking in the song his mother is singing,

as cattle brand, as thumbprint whorl,
as flooded river eddying back on itself.

When Jean-François Pilâtre, first man
to go up in a hot air balloon, looked down

into the wind-diced Seine, he saw only
a sliver of the balloon reflected back,

the shadow of his gondola, his own small
body, suspended as if by nothing.

Lightly at First, Then Rapture

"I would not say that the future is necessarily less predictable than the past. I think the past was not predictable when it started."
—Donald Rumsfeld

Beyond the blue chalk line
of the highway, acreage
of corn, stalks cuckolding
one another in the wind.
Closer, the yard crusts
over with rotten plums;
a delirium of squirrels
natters in the upper limbs.
And here in the kitchen
the dishwasher jet thuds
its muted round, too like
the sonogram heartbeat.
When the washer finishes,
even sound will abandon
this house. Each dawn
is a piece of dark flint
hefted under dim light.
But not to worry. My
neighbor tells me that
any time now, an angel
will sound a few notes
on its bleating trumpet.
Jesus will poke the divine
straw into the atmosphere
and suck the righteous
up to heaven, their bodies
jangling like pennies
through the Hoover tube.
Whether we're taken
or not, says my neighbor.

The Sad Truth about Rilke's Poems

—for Julia and Robert

The man feeding ducks throws out only one crust
    at a time no matter how
        many birds crowd the water.
All of Picasso's lovers want their breasts and ears back.

    We live on separate
        islands. Every night we meet
in boats on the star-dusted slate of water and watch
    each other speak. You don't
        hear the creaking oarlocks.

Rilke's poems are so much less lovely in German.
    When painting a bird, Prévert says, you must
            start
by painting a cage. John Cage just sits at the piano.

    In translation, something
        of beauty always dies,
but something also is carried over. A word unlovely
    as a fifty-year-old nail can dance
        in your hands.

Isn't it funny how the mouth makes the same shape
    to say *auricle* and *oracle*? The voice is
        a trembling of the body so minute
that only the air can feel it. You must watch closely.

Rilke's done writing poems. Too many
        people close
their eyes to listen to your singing, as if it was the light
    of the fire that burns
        and not the heat at the heart of it.

"Of the last peeces of Painters"

*". . . for in these and such like imperfect tables, man may (as it were)
see what traicts and lineaments remayne to bee done, as also the very
dessiegnes and cogitations of the Artificers . . . so the conceit that they be
now dead and missing, is no small griefe unto us, when wee behold them
so raw and fore-let."*—Pliny the Elder

1. Leonardo's *Adoration of the Magi* (begun 1481)

The trees leach each photon from the ruined
basilica. Inside a singularity, say the magi,
miracles are possible. This is the star we
followed: not a glittering chip of light, but
a gut-ache darkness, a hole bored straight
through the world we know. The universe
began this way: baobab trees, El Caminos,
swallowed baby teeth, comets, infidelity,
salmon leaping clean of sparkled water, all
condensed to a single point. The horsemen
go on rearing and fighting in the middle distance.
The world, the magi say, is collapsing again.
Mary, ghost-sketched, holds out her finished son.

2. Ryugyong Hotel, North Korea (begun 1987)

The postage stamps depict a completed hotel
but were issued before the building was half
finished. Today, to post a letter with such
a stamp is an act of sedition. At midnight,
the eight hundred statues of Kim Il-Sung
shake their heads in despair. An unknown
species of heron nests in the penthouses,
the creaking notes of their mating song
fluttering down one hundred five stories

like propaganda leaflets. Ornithologists
have noted the birds congregate beneath
the construction crane fixed to the spire.
The meaning of this behavior is unknown.
Some say the birds gather simply to enjoy
fresh air. Others claim the birds have begun
to worship the crane, that the notes drifting
down to the street below are in fact prayers.

3. Bruce Lee's *Game of Death* (begun 1973)

If our bodies swap out ninety-eight percent
of their atoms every year, who can complain
about a stand-in filling out our abandoned
storylines? What we hoped would exhibit
our grace becomes just another chop-socky
flick, our own funeral just stock footage
for the character's faked death. Yes, but
we are still reborn, new identities carved
into our faces, wraparound shades to hide
our unfamiliar eyes when we look into
the mirror. And the many-tiered pagoda
full of kung fu henchmen: isn't it as good
a metaphor of the afterlife as any scale
of featherweight hearts or chasm bridges
that narrow in proportion to our wickedness?
After each flight of stairs we find another
fighter bouncing on his feet, ready to do us in.

4. Jimi Hendrix's *First Rays of the New Rising Sun* (begun 1970)

Remember the first night jumps, your faith
in the parachute still unsteady, the seam
between heaven and earth barely visible,
your bones rattling like a snare drum.
You thought it might be god who lived

in a room walled with mirrors, god who
every night kneeled in front of his own
image, soaked the instruments of creation
in lighter fluid and set the world on fire.
When the door opens, the pressure drop
tugs at your skin. When it's your time
to die, you're the one who has to do it.

5. Nikolai Gogol's *Dead Souls* (begun 1835)

The defendant picked over lifetimes of garbage
for bank statements and gas bills. From beeps
overheard in line at the ATM, he learned
his neighbors' PINs. The social security cards
he purchased from the lean grandsons of recently
deceased dowagers. The stolen identities
he assembled, a hundred in all, lived together
in his one-bedroom efficiency, stacked
in lumpy bunk beds. The arresting officers
said they'd never seen anything like it.
Men and women, some decades dead, lay
breast to back, some smoking thin cigarettes,
some poring over scraps of old newspaper.
In court, he held up a copy of Gogol's great,
unfinished novel. I invite you to look, he read,
more closely into your duty and the obligation
of your earthly service for we all have as yet
but a dim understanding of it, and we scarcely

Notes Regarding Things We Know

Of Philemon Holland's 1634 translation of Pliny's *Natural History,* Richard T. Bruere writes, "When clarity called for amplification or paraphrase Holland did not hesitate; his amplifications however are designed to convey the precise intention of his author, not to exhibit his own cleverness, and enlighten rather than disgust." *The Cambridge History of English and American Literature* (1907–1921) adds of Holland, "His was the romance not of feeling, but of decoration. He loved ornament with the ardour of an ornamental age, and he tricked out his authors with all the resources of Elizabethan English. The concision and reticence of the classics were as nothing to him. He was ambitious always to clothe them in the garb which they might have worn had they been not mere Englishmen, but fantastics of his own age." Among the probable progenitors of the question mark are the exclamation point and the semicolon—that is, either a shout or a pause. The sea anemone has a single opening that serves as both its mouth and anus. The claim that Grigori Aleksandrovich Potemkin erected fake villages along the Dnieper River to impress Catherine the Great is likely untrue or, at best, an exaggeration. According to the Federal Railroad Administration, roughly 800 individuals were killed by trains in 2007. The Office of Safety Analysis lists several codes for these fatalities, including: "Struck by object," "Highway-rail collision/impact," "Struck by on-track equipment," "Slipped, fell, stumbled, other," "Struck against object," "Lost balance," "Assaulted by other," "Sudden, unexpected movement," and "Other (describe in narrative)." Before he was killed by a soldier, Archimedes said, "Do not disturb my circles." Bees dance in the air to direct their fellow bees to nectar. The Gordian worm, a parasitic nematomorph, matures inside the host cricket, and then invades the insect's brain, causing it to seek out water and drown itself, at which point the worm will escape. Darwin did not at first recognize that the Galapagos finches were related to one another. Regarding the rapture, 1 Corinthians 15:51–54, has this to say: "Behold, I tell you a mystery: We shall not all sleep, but we shall all be changed—in a moment, in the twinkling of an eye, at the last trumpet. For the trumpet will sound, and the dead will be raised incorruptible, and we shall be changed. For this corruptible must put on incorruption, and this mortal must put on immortality. So when this corruptible has put on incorruption, and this mortal has put on immortality, then shall be brought to pass the saying that is written: 'Death is swallowed up in victory.'" Gogol burned the remainder of *Dead Souls,* most likely at the urging of a religious zealot. Three-quarters of a million people were killed at the Third Battle of Ypres in 1917. Mustard gas was used there for the first time. The already marshy land was so distressed by bombardment that many soldiers were lost in stretches of liquid mud several feet deep. The olm is a blind, cave-dwelling amphibian. Paracelsus, noted sixteenth-century alchemist, said, "All things are poison and nothing is without poison, only the dose permits something not to be poisonous." The ratio of pigs to humans in the world is roughly 1 to 6. When scientists exhumed Petrarch's skeleton in 2003, a DNA test of a rib and a tooth revealed two interesting facts: (1) the skull was not Petrarch's and (2) it was a woman's skull. Rilke wrote, "I am so afraid of people's words." In fact, many man-made structures are visible from space, including highways and stadiums. The so-called Old Man of the Lake is a large tree that has been floating vertically in Crater Lake for over 100 years. To the dismay of his colleagues, Harry Harlow insisted on giving gruesome names to the devices he created for experimenting on rhesus monkeys: the Iron Maiden, the Rape Rack, the Pit of Despair. Of his isolation experiments, he wrote, "The effects of 6 months of total social isolation were so devastating and debilitating that we had assumed initially that 12 months of isolation would not produce any additional decrement. This assumption proved to be false; 12 months of isolation almost obliterated the animals socially." Storks are mute. The belief that rain follows the plow—that is, that agricultural cultivation generates increased rainfall—was popular through the end of the nineteenth century. The Portuguese word *saudade* denotes a longing for a fondly remembered person or thing that has been lost; it also implies the acknowledgment, however deeply buried, that the beloved person or thing will never return. The word has no direct equivalent in any other language. Some varieties of bamboo can grow over three feet per day. When Dr. Irene Pepperberg left Alex—an African Grey Parrot with a vocabulary of over 150 words—with a veterinarian for treatment, Alex vocalized the words, "Come here. I love you. I'm sorry. I want to go back."

Acknowledgments

Gulf Coast: "Of the Parrat and other birds that can speake"
Prairie Schooner: "What Is Not Inside the Head-Sized Box"
    and "Ancient Theories"
Switched-on Gutenberg: "Too Many, Too Few"

I would like to thank the Wisconsin Institute for Creative Writing for their generous support during my time as Jay C. and Ruth Halls Poetry Fellow, 2007–2008. I would also like to thank Carrie Conners, Cynthia Hoffman, and Jesse Lee Kercheval for their invaluable advice and support during the completion of this book.

Nick Lantz is the author of two poetry collections. His first, *We Don't Know We Don't Know,* won the 2009 Katharine Bakeless Nason Prize for Poetry, selected by Linda Gregerson and awarded by Middlebury College and the Bread Loaf Writers' Conference. His second collection, *The Lightning That Strikes the Neighbors' House,* won the Felix Pollak Prize in Poetry. He lives in Madison, Wisconsin.

Bread Loaf and the Bakeless Prizes

The Katharine Bakeless Nason Literary Publication Prizes were established in 1995 to expand the Bread Loaf Writers' Conference's commitment to the support of emerging writers. Endowed by the LZ Francis Foundation, the prizes commemorate Middlebury College patron Katharine Bakeless Nason and launch the publication career of a poet, fiction writer, and a creative nonfiction writer annually. Winning manuscripts are chosen in an open national competition by a distinguished judge in each genre. Winners are published by Graywolf Press.

2009 Judges

Linda Gregerson
Poetry

Percival Everett
Fiction

Sue Halpern
Creative Nonfiction

This book was designed by Connie Kuhnz. It is set in Minion Pro by BookMobile Design and Publishing Services, and manufactured by Versa Press on acid-free paper.